World of
the Reptiles

A Cherrytree Book

Designed and produced by
A S Publishing

First published 1988
by Cherrytree Press Ltd
a subsidiary of
The Chivers Company Ltd
Windsor Bridge Road
Bath, Avon BA2 3AX

Copyright © Cherrytree Press Ltd 1988

British Library Cataloguing in Publication Data

Head, John G.
　World of the reptiles.—(The Ages of
　Earth)
　1. Prehistoric organisms – For children
　I. Title II. Robinson, Bernard, *1930-*
　III. Series
　560

　ISBN 0-7451-5013-6

Printed in Hong Kong by Colorcraft Ltd

All rights reserved. No part of this publication may be reproduced, stored in a retrieval system, or transmitted, in any form or by any means without the prior permission in writing of the publisher, nor be otherwise circulated in any form of binding or cover other than that in which it is published and without a similar condition including this condition being imposed on the subequent purchaser.

THE AGES OF EARTH

World of the Reptiles

By John G. Head
Illustrated by Bernard Robinson

CHERRYTREE BOOKS

The Space-Time Shuttle was about to land – in the Permian Period, some 275 million years ago. It was on the third stage of its prehistoric tour. A place for two on this tour had been the first prize in a competition for children all over the world.

Mike, the lucky winner, was on board, along with his sister Helen. Helen had not really wanted to come. She saw nothing in being frightened half to death by prehistoric monsters. They had met some too in their first few stops. But Helen had surprised everyone by her bravery. When Jen, their Space-Time Ranger, had fallen into a swamp, Helen had risked her life to save her.

Now they were safe inside the Shuttle. It was dark outside because the craft was travelling through time.

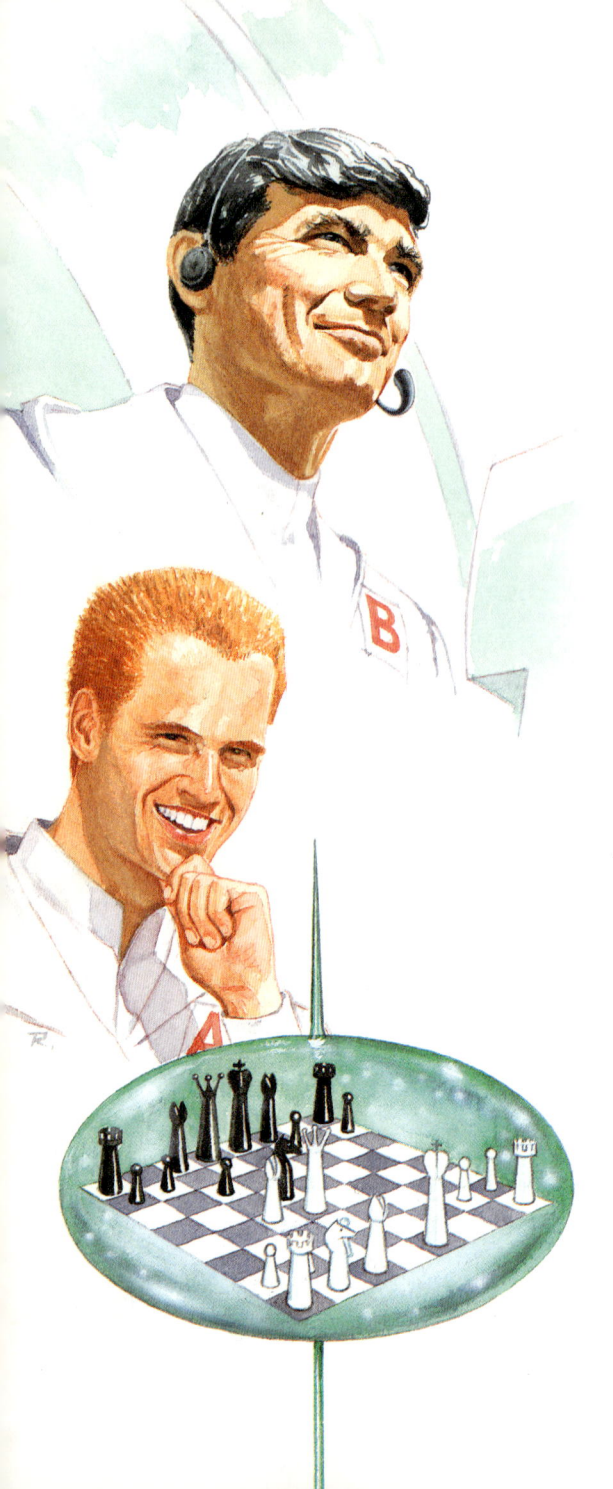

Captain Marsh – Bob – was on the flight deck. Lieutenant 'Atty' Atkins was playing chess with Timcom, the computer. Jen, Mike and Helen were discussing the swamp. Jen had fallen into the swamp while trying to get closer to an animal that Mike had thought was a reptile. She was desperate to see a reptile. The first reptiles had evolved during the Carboniferous period but so far they had seen only amphibians.

'What's so special about reptiles?' asked Helen. 'They look the same as amphibians to me.'
'No, they are quite different,' replied Jen. 'Reptiles have scaly skins that stop their bodies drying out in the heat. They don't have to stay by water like amphibians.'
'I suppose if Timcom didn't have to play chess all the time,' said Helen, 'we might get a look at a reptile.'

The computer responded instantly. A hologram of Hylonomus, one of the earliest known reptiles, appeared on the screen. Timcom told them all about the creature – and at the same time planned his next move.

6

Hylonomus
(a Carboniferous
amphibian)

'The most important thing about reptiles apart from their skins,' said Timcom, 'is their eggs. They have hard shells. The shells stop the eggs drying out, so the animals can lay them on land, and –'

'Oh, shoot!' exploded Atty. 'That computer beats me every time, even when he's not concentrating.'

'He's not a he, he's an it,' chided Helen.

'Not the sort of it I want to play with,' sulked Atty.

The seat belt sign flashed on. It was late morning when the Shuttle landed.

'Today,' said Jen, 'we are going to see some reptiles.'

'But not,' said Bob, 'if it kills you. It nearly did last time.'

'We'll look after her,' said Mike and Helen, as they set off.

The three of them were wearing lesion-proof suits and helmets, to protect them from wild animals and from any unknown germs that might attack them. They were connected by intercom and camera to Timcom who monitored their movements and could summon help if they got into trouble.

'Let's head for that lake,' said Jen.

The lake was surrounded by ferns and trees, but smaller ones than the giants they had seen in the Carboniferous Period.

'The climate is much drier now,' said Jen. 'There's not so much water, so the plants don't grow so tall. The ground is dry, too, thank goodness.'

Diplocaulus

'But there aren't any animals,' said Helen.

'Oh, yes, there are,' said Mike. 'Look at that fellow under the water. He looks like Napoleon.'

'That is Diplocaulus,' said Timcom over the intercom. 'It's an amphibian, not a reptile.'

'And look over there,' said Mike, hearing a splash. A fat beast, two metres long and almost as wide, was lumbering out of the water, with a fish clenched in its jaws. It was rather like a hippo.

'That's an Eryops,' said Jen and Timcom together.

'There's another one in the water,' said Mike. 'They look very fierce.'

'Don't worry,' said Helen, 'with a gut like that, I bet they can't move very fast.'

Eryops

Cacops

But nobody was taking any chances. When the Eryops in the water turned in their direction, they took to their heels and didn't stop until they were safe on top of a ridge that the lumbering amphibians certainly couldn't reach.

Away from the lake the land was red and rocky. Clumps of conifers and scrubby ferns provided patches of green.

'You realize where you are, don't you?' asked Jen.

'In the Permian Period,' said Mike.

'That's *when* you are. *Where* you are is Texas,' said Jen. 'We could be standing where Dallas is today.'

They lolled on the ground and watched the insects in the ferns.

Diadectes

They were still big but not as big as the Carboniferous ones.
'The creatures eating them are called Cacops,' whispered Jen, before Timcom had a chance to identify them.

'What's that huge thing over there?' asked Helen, pointing to an amphibian that was even bigger than the Eryops. It was feeding on the lower fronds of a seed fern, like a contented deer.
'That is a Diadectes,' said Timcom.

Watching the Diadectes happily munching made them feel hungry, so after a while they tramped back to the Shuttle for lunch. They were disappointed not to have seen any reptiles, so Bob suggested that they move on in time.

While they were eating, the Shuttle soundlessly moved on 20 million years to the middle of the Permian Period. When they landed, the landscape looked much the same, though even drier. They were still in Texas.

Jen, Mike and Helen set out again, climbing up the steep walls of a river canyon to get a good view. Strange shapes appeared on the tops of the cliffs above them.

'What on earth are those? asked Mike. 'Can we climb up and see?'

'We can try,' said Jen, who had a pretty good idea what the shapes were. Fortunately, they were out of range of Timcom's cameras so he couldn't give the game away.

After an hour they stopped. It was hard going and Helen refused to go any farther.

'You are really mean,' said Mike. 'I'm going on alone.'

'No, you are not,' snapped Timcom.

'Yes,' said Jen. 'Timcom's right. It's far too dangerous and we promised that we wouldn't split up.'

'Look, look!' yelled Helen suddenly. She had wandered off to avoid a row.

The row was soon forgotten. Helen had found a nest. It had four eggs in it. They all crowded round to look.

'I wonder who laid them,' said Jen.

A growl from behind a rock told her soon enough.

'Help!' screamed Helen, as a huge shape sprang towards her.

Ophiacodon

Mike was quickest on the draw with his stun gun. The dart hit the creature in mid-leap and it thudded to the ground.

'Let's get out of here,' said Jen, pushing the children ahead of her.

'That was Ophiacodon,' said Timcom, 'a carnivorous reptile.'

'I wanted to *see* a reptile,' said Jen, 'not be eaten by one.'

They scrambled down the rocks until they were on open ground within sight of the Shuttle. Skirting some trees they heard a strange, scuffling sound. Helen and Jen began to run, but Mike was too curious. He crept towards the sound and called the others back. He had found another nest. This time there were four baby reptiles in it.

'Those look as if they belong to another of those things that sprang at us,' said Jen, forcing Mike to come away.

Mike did as he was told, but kept looking backwards as he walked. Jen and Helen were in deep conversation, so they did not notice how far behind them Mike was trailing. Nor did they hear the squealing noise that made him stop and retrace his steps.

Too scared to go all the way back to the nest, he peered over the edge of some rocks.

A huge creature with a great sail on its back had attacked the nest. Even now it was eating one of the little reptiles. The others had managed to escape. Mike watched in amazement and horror.

The animal was two and a half metres long. Its sail, catching the last rays of sunlight, was as high as a tree. Its teeth were long and sharp. Mike was close enough to hear it ripping through its little victim's flesh and crunching its bones.

Mike felt safe enough behind the rocks. The huge predator was busy eating, and would not catch Mike's scent through his suit. But it was getting dark and Mike was getting frightened.

Soon the animal left its meal and lumbered back to a crevice in the rocks. Mike knew that the others would be searching for him, so he made sure he could not be seen. He switched off his intercom and gently scrambled over the rocks and crept towards a boulder near the destroyed nest. He was quaking with fear, but determined.

Dimetrodon
(a pelycosaur)

One of the little creatures that had got away was cowering under the rock. Quietly, Mike approached. The creature could not see him. As gently as he could, Mike seized the little beast.

'Now you're safe,' he said to it. 'You are coming with me.'
'Now you are safe,' said a loud voice in the darkness. 'You are coming with me.' It was Atty, who had hurried to find Mike as soon as the girls arrived back without him. He was furious.
'You are not bringing that creature aboard the Shuttle,' said Atty. 'So don't even ask.'
'I'm not going without it,' said Mike. 'If I leave it, it will be killed.'

When they reached the Shuttle, the Captain refused to open the hatch. Mike refused to leave his new pet. Eventually Jen put on her suit and went outside to talk to him. She felt guilty at having lost him on the way back.

'Mike, you can only do the creature harm by taking him with us,' she said. 'He belongs here, even if he is eaten by another pelycosaur,' she said.

'What's a pelycosaur?' asked Mike, sulkily.

'It's a kind of reptile,' said Jen. 'That Dimetrodon you saw with the sail-back is a pelycosaur. I wish I'd seen it. I knew there were pelycosaurs about, as soon as you spotted those shapes on the cliffs.'

'It was amazing,' said Mike, proud that he alone had seen the monster. 'It was this big.'

Mike spread his arms to show the size of the Dimetrodon, and the little fellow in his arms leapt to freedom. Mike set off after him but skidded to a halt. There was another sail-back in his path. He fled back to the Shuttle as fast as his legs would carry him.

Edaphosaurus (a pelycosaur)

'Serves you right!' said Bob, as he helped Mike and Jen aboard. 'You deserved a fright.'

'You wouldn't have got one,' laughed Helen, 'if your intercom had been switched on. Timcom would have told you that the reptile you ran away from was an Edaphosaurus, a harmless plant-eater.'

'The little beast you rescued was probably an Ophiacodon, like the creature that attacked us,' said Jen in an attempt to cheer Mike up. 'He'd have starved to death if he'd come with us. We couldn't have fed him. Carnivores don't like their food squeezed out of tubes.'

But Mike would not be cheered up. He went to talk to Timcom. The computer told him all about the strange sail-backs: how they used their sails like radiators, standing side on to the sun to warm up, and end on to cool down. Soon everyone else went to bed. So Mike went, too, sadly wondering what fate had befallen his reptilian friend.

'Last stop in the Permian,' said Atty in the morning. 'If anyone wants to go out, they are to stay within fifty metres of the Shuttle. And nobody, repeat nobody, is ever to switch off their intercom – Mike.'
'Let's stay in the craft today,' said Jen.
'Okay, we'll hover,' said the obliging Atty.

Everyone gathered round the hatches to watch the scene below. The landscape was much greener. The ferns looked almost like grass. Feeding on the ground cover was a vast herd of reptiles, identified as Dicynodons by Timcom.

Dicynodon

Dicynodon

They stopped the craft by a water hole, where a couple of Dicynodons were bathing. A family of Moschops was grazing nearby.

'Let's go out,' pleaded Mike. 'It's no fun inside.'

'You could go out,' said Timcom, 'if you want to take your chances with that Lycaenops.'

They all gaped as a lion-like creature got ready to spring. A young Moschops who had straggled away from its companions was the victim. The slow little plant-eater didn't stand a chance.

'You see what happens, Mike,' said Bob, 'when you stray.'

Mike was too upset by the violent scene outside the window to take any more teasing. He fought back his tears.

'Can we go somewhere else, please?' he asked.

Moschops

Lycaenops

'Don't be upset, Mike,' said his sister. 'The Lycaenops has to eat, too.'

The Shuttle hovered away from the water hole. It was time for lunch, but Mike wouldn't eat. He went to talk to Timcom. Timcom knew all about the Lycaenops.

'It is rather like a big cat, you see,' said the computer. 'It can run faster than all the other Permian animals because its legs are stronger. They are under its body. They don't stick out at the sides like a lizard's. You try walking like a lizard. You won't go very fast.'

Mike laughed. Fancy a computer cheering you up!

'Look at the screen,' said Timcom, 'and I'll show you something special.'

Cynognathus

On the holoscreen was a small creature, a reptile about the size of a cat. It had rough hair over its back.

'What's so special about that?' asked Mike, disappointed.

'That is a mammal-like reptile, called Cynognathus. The difference between reptiles and mammals is the ability of mammals to keep warm even in cold weather. Their hair helps them to keep warm. This is one of the first hairy animals. It's a forerunner of the mammals, the greatest creatures ever to live on earth.'

'I thought dinosaurs were the greatest creatures,' said Mike.

'No,' said Timcom. 'They were the biggest land animals, but mammals are much more important.'

'I'd love to see a live hairy reptile,' said Jen. 'Can we go and fine one?'

'We can,' said Bob, 'but I was hoping to move on to the Triassic period today. It would be nice to see a dinosaur.'

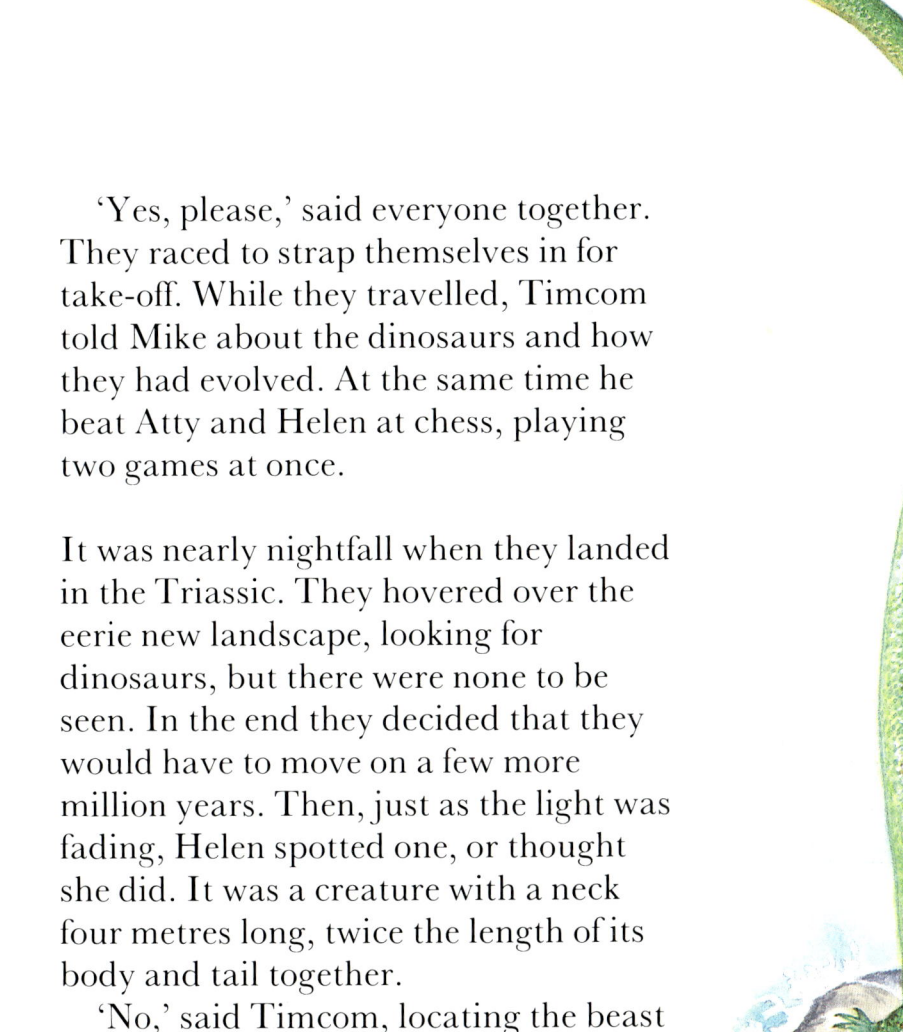

'Yes, please,' said everyone together. They raced to strap themselves in for take-off. While they travelled, Timcom told Mike about the dinosaurs and how they had evolved. At the same time he beat Atty and Helen at chess, playing two games at once.

It was nearly nightfall when they landed in the Triassic. They hovered over the eerie new landscape, looking for dinosaurs, but there were none to be seen. In the end they decided that they would have to move on a few more million years. Then, just as the light was fading, Helen spotted one, or thought she did. It was a creature with a neck four metres long, twice the length of its body and tail together.

'No,' said Timcom, locating the beast she had seen. 'That is not a dinosaur. It's a Tanystropheus. It uses that long neck for fishing.'

Tanystropheus

Megazostrodons

Mike was first up in the morning. The Shuttle had landed long before dawn. He persuaded Bob to let him and Jen go out to explore as soon as there was a glimmer of light.

Promising to stay within a hundred metres of the Shuttle, Jen and Mike set off. They walked through the undergrowth on the edge of what looked like a large forest. They found nothing except for a few scuttling lizards. Mike had been expecting to see great herds of dinosaurs. Suddenly he spotted a little animal like the Cynognathus that Timcom had shown him. This time it was a real mammal called Megazostrodon. It had a long nose and whiskers, and was snapping up insects.

Jen was really excited. Megazostrodon was one of the very first mammals. She made Mike sit quite still for ages, until another one came out.

Mike was disappointed. They had gone as far as they were allowed and they'd seen only these boring mammals.

'I can see animals like that back home,' said Mike. He stomped back to the Shuttle. Jen followed. It was only when they had climbed into the craft that they saw what they had missed. On the ground was a trail of freshly made footprints. They were the tracks of a dinosaur called Coelophysis. Helen had spotted it from the window of the Shuttle. Mike was furious.

Coelophysis

Dilosophaurus

Plateosaurus

'Quickly,' said Helen. 'We've been waiting for you so that we can follow the dinosaur. It runs awfully fast.' Bob put the Shuttle into hover mode, and zoomed after the speedy dinosaur. It was nowhere to be seen, so they parked the craft and discussed what to do next. They were interrupted by Timcom. Its camera had picked up a large dinosaur called Plateosaurus. They rushed to the windows.

A heavy beast, some six metres long, was lumbering towards them. It stopped fifty metres from the Shuttle to browse on a maidenhair tree. Then, suddenly, a flesh-eating dinosaur called Dilophosaurus appeared, speeding towards the plant-eater.

It struck at the huge beast with its claws and snapped at its neck. Too big to run, the Plateosaurus sank to the ground. The Dilophosaurus ripped its scaly flesh, and it roared with pain. Mike shut his eyes. Seeing dinosaurs wasn't quite as nice as he had thought.

'Don't worry,' said Atty, 'I'll soon stop that.' He started the Shuttle engines. The Dilophosaurus was terrified of the noise and sped away from its victim.
'Thanks, Atty,' said Mike. 'I'd have hated my first dinosaur to be a dead one!'

THE AGES OF EARTH TOUR

Shuttle back in time and see with your own eyes 600 million years of Earth's history in just three weeks.

Periods	Years Ago (Millions)	Plants and Animals
Pre-cambrian Time	4500	No life on Earth to start with. Tiny plants appear about 3000 million years ago in the sea; first known animals appear about 700 million years ago.

PALAEOZOIC ERA

Periods	Years Ago (Millions)	Plants and Animals
Cambrian	600	No life on land, but in the sea there are creatures called graptolites and trilobites, corals and sponges, shellfish and jellyfish.
Ordovician	500	More graptolites and trilobites in sea. Creatures called brachiopods and the first fish — which have armour.
Silurian	440	Land plants appear. Lots of fish in the sea and giant sea-scorpions.
Devonian	395	The age of fishes. Sea teems with all kinds, including huge jawed fish and sharks. Small creatures leave the sea to live on land. Amphibians evolve from fish.
Carboniferous	345	Giant land plants in coal swamps. Large amphibians and the first insects, including some giants. Reptiles evolve from amphibians.
Permian	280	Lots more reptiles and fewer amphibians. Trilobites die out.

THE AGES OF EARTH TOUR

Visit each of these periods and see the animals and plants of bygone ages, monsters of land and sea and sky.

	Periods	Years Ago (Millions)	Plants and Animals
MESOZOIC ERA	Triassic	225	The first dinosaurs. Large reptiles and shelled creatures called ammonites in the sea. Mammals evolve from reptiles.
	Jurassic	200	Lots of dinosaurs, including huge sauropods and carnosaurs. Pterosaurs in the air. Birds evolve from reptiles.
	Cretaceous	135	New kinds of dinosaurs, including ones with armour. Small mammals and birds. First flowering plants. At the end of the period dinosaurs and many other creatures die out.
CENOZOIC ERA	Tertiary	65	The age of mammals. Many kinds of mammals evolve, including horses, elephants and apes. Coniferous forests and grasslands.
	Quaternary	2	Mammoths, woolly rhinos and sabre-toothed cats live through Ice Ages. Ancestors of humans evolve from apes. The first humans appear.

Index

Ammonites 31
Amphibians 6, 9, 10, 11, 30
Animals, evolution of 30, 31
Apes 31
Armoured fish 30

Birds 31
Brachiopods 30

Cacops 10, 11
Cambrian Period 30
Carboniferous Period 30
Carnosaurs 31
Cenozoic Era 31
Coal swamps 30
Coelophysis 27
Coniferous forests 31
Conifers 10
Corals 30
Cretaceous Period 31
Cynognathus 24, 26

Devonian Period 30
Diadectes 11
Dicynodons 21, 22
Dimetrodon 17, 19
Dinosaurs 24, 25, 29, 31
Diplocaulus 8, 9

Earth, history of 30, 31
Edaphosaurus 19, 20
Elephants 31
Eryops 9-11
Evolution 30, 31

Ferns 8, 10
Fish 30

Graptolites 30
Grassland 31

Horses 31
Humans, ancestors of 31
Hylonomus 7

Ice Ages 31
Insects 10, 30

Jawed fish 30
Jellyfish 30
Jurassic Period 31

Lizards 23
Lycaenops 22, 23

Mammal-like reptile 24
Mammals 24, 26, 27, 31
Mammoths 31
Megazostradon 26
Mesozoic Era 31
Moschops 22

Ophiacodon 13, 14, 20
Ordovician Period 30

Palaeozoic Era 30
Pelycosaur 17, 19
Permian Period 5, 10, 12, 21, 23, 30
Plants 8, 31
Plateosaurus 29
Pre-cambrian times 30
Pterosaurs 31

Quaternary Period 31

Reptiles 6, 7, 9, 11, 14-16, 24, 30, 31

Sabre-toothed cats 31
Sauropods 31
Sea-scorpions 30
Seed fern 11
Sharks 30
Shellfish 30
Silurian Period 30
Sponges 30

Tanystropheus 25
Tertiary Period 31
Texas 10, 12
Trees 8
Triassic Period 25, 31
Trilobites 30

Woolly rhinos 31